PHASING

Freely

Phasing Freely

Phasing Freely
By: Tyler Lenn Bradley

ISBN: 9798988174646

Published by Alegria Publishing

Table of Contents

New Moon

My Genesis

Waxing Crescent

Dominoes
Scene 1: Rocking Chair
Question 1
Scene 2: Rocking Chair (Reprise)
Absorption
y = mx + b
Enmeshment
Unseen
Vased
My Depression's Mantra

First Quarter

Synthesis

Waxing Gibbous

Swing
Consumed
Vital Deceit
Conform
White Figures
Scene 3: A Negro Woman
Expectations
To Do
Caged
In a small café in Rome, there is a woman...
Question 2
Trigger Tales

Full Moon

Luminous Truth

Waning Gibbous

A Daughter like Me
The Alphabet
Notified Worth
Question 3
Plastic
Choose Wisely
To: My Former Doctors
Pussy Peace
Scene 4: I AM
Twenty Words

Last Quarter

you fill my little spot

Waning Crescet

Promise to Myself
Breathe
WOMEN SHIT
Ant Advice
Choices
Selective Shopping
Wisdom
Atoms & More and More
Question 4
My Self-Love Mantra

New Moon

Be like the Moon

Afterward

Luna, My Love Lyrics

Content Disclosure
The individual poems in this collection do not have a content warning. The following topics will be addressed in this book: domestic violence, depression, anxiety, self-harm, and suicidal ideation.

Content Invitation
The individual poems in this collection were written in the hopes of inspiring vulnerability. Please be prepared for the potential desire to do the following: reflect, accept, heal, affirm, and love yourself.

Phasing Freely

New Moon

I am anew
a new breath
new presence
a blank canvas
just given life
wandering eyes
observant
unharmed
and unarmed
waiting
to release
to become
to transform.

My Genesis

In the beginning, there was nothing.
Nothing but slight swirls of light
awakening novice, eager eyes.
Nothing but an untouched mind
waiting to discover an unknown world
and that unknown world seemed good.

And then the unknown world said
Let there be familial love.
And so, there was familial love
and the untouched mind was
immersed in precious, timeless love
and that love was pure and good.

And then familial love said
Let there be generational trauma.
And so, there was generational trauma
and the untouched mind unconsciously
inhaled that potent ancestral trauma
and that trauma was ever present and good.

And then the traumatized said
Let there be perfection.
And so, there was perfection
and the traumatized saw how perfection
brought pride and purpose to their lives
and so, the new mind learned that perfection was good.

And then perfection said
Let there be fear.
And so, there was fear
and that fear spiraled into every crevice
of the developing mind's vibrations and dreams
and that fear flourished within the mind for good.

And then fear said
Let there be judgment.
And so, there was judgment
and the developing mind became
possessed by biased judgements of others
and to the judges that was good.

And then judgment said
Let there be anxiety.
And so, there was anxiety
and that anxiety secretly controlled
the developing mind with riddles for decades
and that anxiety became persistent and good.

And then anxiety said
Let there be depression.
And so, there was depression
and that depression slowly, but patiently
consumed the developing mind's every being
and that depression grew powerful, purposeful,
and good.

And then depression said
Let there be death by bridge.
Let this mind jump and try to fly.
Let this mind try to be enough
one last time.
And so, the mind found a bridge
and to depression that was good.

But while on this bridge
awaiting their final flight
on a cold, obsessive night
the mind saw everything:
every mountain, every tree,
every star, everything in sight
including the moon.

And then the moon said
Let there be light.
And the mind willingly absorbed
the splendor, the radiance of hope
glistening in the moon's light
and that hope was good.

And so, the story goes
for this mind, there was no death
no deadly jump or flight.

Instead, there was this mighty book
and that was *truly* good.

Dearest Human,

I have lived a good life. A life full of love, joy, smiles - a life of happiness. But even so, somehow, I've suffered from anxiety, depression, and suicidal ideation. Why? Now that's quite the question. A question I've been patiently and gently answering through therapy. A question that I will probably be answering for the rest of my life.

But isn't it interesting? The human experience, I mean. We begin as these new beings, these blank canvases in a way and then what? The world! The world, like an enchanted, incessant paint brush, covers us with experiences, people, trials, joys, tears, laughs – and most of these things we don't get to choose.

And then we become us.

I wrote this book to explore my "us." This book is a collection of poems, quotes, and journal prompts, and more - some I have written and others I was gifted. I wrote it for me, but I also wrote it for you. I hope that in reading my story you'll learn to find the moon beyond your bridge too. My journey is yours to explore. Take what you need, but please leave and respect what you don't. This is my truth. This is my story. I hope it helps you.

With Love,
Tyler Lenn Bradley

Phasing Freely

Waxing Crescent

I am absorbing
a saturated
sopping sponge
swallowing
ancestral life
consuming trauma
without control
or consent
cramming
learning to
stow
bury
hide.

Dominoes

my ancestors
fought the war so,
I wouldn't have to.

way down in the
trench
of despair, gasping
for air
a battleground
fought with
perseverance and
prayer.

bombs blasting
tear gas casting
cries of slaves
seemed
everlasting.

but my ancestors
fought the war
so, I wouldn't have
to.

my grans fought
the battle
so, I wouldn't have
to.

revolution was
their game
troops and soldiers
of freedom
blackness
they reclaimed.

sirens
shrieking
lynch trees
creaking
calls for equality
were peaking.

but my grans
fought the battle
so, I wouldn't have
to.

I fight the fight so,
my descendants
won't have to.

my fight lives
inside
depression the
new
oppression whips
and
mines of the mind.

slaves were raped
warriors escaped,
but
chains of my
ancestors
found a new
shape.

but I fight the
fight
so, my
descendants won't
have to.

slav·er·y

/ˈslāv(ə)rē/

noun

a domino effect expressed in different ways.

Scene 1: Rocking Chair

Center Stage: A single, weathered, rocking chair sits alone in a dim lingering spotlight.

ENTER – YOUNG WOMAN.

YOUNG WOMAN gently approaches the chair. With each step she transforms into her mother. She sits. Her mother speaks.

YOUNG WOMAN:
Some people have the need to move
they crave the spark that engages their veins
the muscles that tense and ignite like a flame
they love the feeling a beat can sustain
they love the sound and music of the rain.

But me?
I used to move to help get through my pain.
My rocking chair was my movements' chains.
I'd sit in its small wooden frame
and rock every day to escape my disdain.

My rocking chair kept me alive.
Its wooden limbs
were small and fine
not expensive or divine
but I rocked to survive.
I was only five.

But it helped me hide
escape the cries
the lies
and my father's bloodshot eyes.

My father who seemed divine
at least from the outside
an ex-marine, chemist, smart, tall
he loved the sound of jazz
playing through the hall
but alcohol was his downfall.

And as night creeped
the garage door would squeak
and I'd open my door
to get a good peak.
He'd storm through the door
tequila dripping from his veins
his soul possessed, his soul in chains
his hands would grasp my mother's skin.

His fist would be crisp
and she'd slam to the floor
her blood streaming down
their bedroom door.

My sister would rush to her aid
only six of age.
She'd bite, kick, and scream
but he'd slap her so loud
it would haunt my dreams.

Then silence would fall
and like the eye of a storm
you could hear nothing at all.
He'd slip away.

"Back to work," he'd say.
My mother's blood I would clean
this was my childhood
my daily routine.

So, I learned to hide in my room
the smallest of them all
but with my rocking chair
I felt 10 feet tall.
I would call on God to help me heal.
I would call on God to make a deal.

God
what do I need to do
to make this horror untrue?
I'll sacrifice anything to you.
And in my mind, I'd hear God say:

GOD:
[A celestial voice from above]

My child, your rocking chair is the only way.
If you rock 1,000 times
you won't have to see the pain in your mother's eyes.
You won't have to see your father's bloodshot eyes
and when he sips,
there'll be no alcohol on his lips.

YOUNG WOMAN:
God, is this true?
No response would come through
but I'd start rocking.

But the pain would never end
every day he would rise again.
And as the night creeped
the alcohol creaked
and leaked
consumed his mind.
His transformation was like
Dr. Jekyll and Mr. Hyde
like the devil, he would arise

and the cries would ring and sing through the halls
my sister would fight, but would always fall.
My mother's blood I would clean
this was my childhood
my daily routine!

Filled with the blood and cries!
The cries
The cries!

God, you lied!
We made a deal!
You promised, it would stop
that it wouldn't be real!

I did what you said
I rocked 1,000 times
every night before bed.

You promised this would not be

but I guess the holy spirit lied to me.

I bet God's lies can kill. Like the quiet temptation of a
pill.

Yes, pills will be fine, pills are kind, I'm only five, but
let me die.
Let me die.

God, please let me die.

Some people have the need to move
away to cope.
They need something when they don't have hope.
Some people do drugs
others cut their skin

some people drown on gin
some people go to church
to confess a sin
and some people can't bear or cope
so, they end their lives
with no hope.

But me? I rocked 1,000 times.
I rocked so hard, I broke a wall
I was hardly three feet tall.

But no one saw me, saw my pain.
They all just walked by and looked away.
No one believed it to be true
but it's easy to ignore something
when it's not happening to you.

I'm older now, I'm grown.
I have a daughter of my own
but before she arrived
my father died.
A heart attack is what they say
but I know he took his life
he gave it away.

My mother became everything she wanted to be.
She is the definition of defying adversity.
My sister grew and her heart is true
but the pain she suffered always
seems to seep through.

Me? I still rock today.
It's a habit that I can't seem
to make go away.
It's a part of me, it's who I am.

But aren't we all shaped by our joys and pains?
We're nothing more than molds of
life experiences that most of us don't get to choose.
So, don't forget that all of this could happen to you too.
It could be happening to the person sitting right next
to you.

So, look around the room
see your peers
and pay attention to their silent tears
to their masks, their cries
their deceptive, deceiving, chameleon eyes.
They need you.

Because there is no politician, no actor, or famous saint
who's going to save people around you from their fate.
But your voice, your love, can do so much more.

So please, take care of the ones around you
because I bet, in their own way
they rock every day too.

Lights fade. YOUNG WOMAN mourns for her mother.

Question 1

Q: How much of my ancestors' trauma lives inside of me?

A: All of it.

For if trauma goes unchecked
It is passed down to the next
Perhaps in a different form
But enough to create a storm.

Scene 2: Rocking Chair (Reprise)

Center Stage: YOUNG WOMAN sits alone in dim timid light. She speaks.

Some people have the need to move
But me?
I move to hide my pain.
My anxiety is my movements' chains.

I twitch and glitch
blink 10 times in a row.
My leg bounces up and down.
I learn fear as I grow.

I keep moving even if I'm ill.
Never let them see you sit still
I was told.

So, I do
all I can
to fit in
and survive
measure
my worth
on how much
I strive.

I
Work
I
Go
I
Achieve
I
Do

I guess in my own way
I rock everyday too.

YOUNG WOMAN remains. Her leg nervously rocks back and forth. Lights fade.

Absorption

Children are sponges.
They absorb everything
in their path, in their sight
without ever knowing
without ever trying.

Every word
Every phrase
Every action

Every joy
Every shame
Every tear

But you can clean a sponge.
You can use warm water
squeeze out the dirty juices
until they disappear, and the
sponge looks almost new.
And then you can begin again

And again
And again
And again

And the sponge
will continue to absorb
without knowing
without a choice
without consent.

Every dirt
Every grease
Every soap

Every waste
Every cleaner
Every crumb from toast.

But then there comes a day
when it's too late
the sponge is done.
It's past the point of cleaning
and it's time
to be replaced.

Children are sponges
but they cannot be replaced.
They cannot disappear
once the dirt from the
world becomes too thick
once the filth from others
creates their fears.
Instead, the grime sits, lingers
and lives on deep inside.

So, be careful what you
let them absorb
what kind of crumbs
you leave on their plate
because one day
the child will realize
that for them
it's much too late.

$$y = mx + b$$

m	x	b	y
I got all A's.	That's what's expected.	12	*Perfection is expected.*
I didn't do well in the game.	That's because you didn't try hard enough.	16	*I am not enough.*
I think I like women.	Where did we go wrong?	19	*I'll just hide it*
My boss bullies me at work.	Women up. It's a good opportunity.	23	*I should just endure.*
I'm moving in with my boyfriend.	You are ungrateful.	27	*What I want is irrelevant.*
I want to travel the world.	You live in LaLa land.	29	*My dreams are frivolous.*
I think I'm depressed.	It's funny how someone who has everything can be depressed.	Unknown	*I'm fine.*

Self = (Vulnerability x Response) + Age

Enmeshment

EveryoneMust
KnowEverything
AboutEveryone
YouTellOne
AndThenThey
TellEveryone
AndIfYouDon't
TellYouAre
Questioned
UntilYouDo
AndThenOnce
YouTellOnce
YouTrust
Someone
TheyTake
YourTruth
AndJudge
ItSoYou
StopSharing
AndThen
Everyone
WondersWhy
ButYouKnow
It'sBecause
YouLearned
AtAnEarly
AgeToHide
YourFeelings
DeepDeep
DeepDeep
DeepDepp
DeepInside.

Unseen

Was I born to serve the holes
in someone else's life?
Is that why I was conceived?
To fill holes made
from dreams unmet
traumas untended
fragile love broken by
years of truths unsaid?

Was I born to be what others need?
To fill hollow holes with
joy that cannot be revived?
To be a love language
the only thing that makes sense
in a fragmented love story?

Was I born to be a
device
mechanism
prop
to hard wire
happiness and pride?

Was I born to become
who *they* wanted to be?
What they desired?
What they craved?
To be a treasure?
A possession?
A dream?

Was I born to serve the holes
in someone else's life?
Or was I just born
with holes of my own
that went *unseen*
by others too busy
filling their holes with **me?**

Vased

Don't pick the flowers

let them be
let them live
let them be free.

Don't pick the flowers

to make them your prize
fertilize your dreams
with a seedling's demise.

Don't pick the flowers

to place them in a vase
filled with synthetic nutrition
for your showcase.

Don't pick the flowers

for the souls that pick
have already been plucked
dreams thrown in muck
pain running amok.

An ever-growing cycle of
picking and plucking
until we're all without soil.
Instead, we
        toil
           boil
              coil
in despair, gasping for air
grasping for the roots
that united us to Mother Earth's
nutrition and care.

Don't pick the flowers

let them be
and then maybe
we'll all be free.

My Depression's Mantra

The boogeyman is me
the one hiding under your bed
the one stalking you at night

waiting
                              patiently

for the right moment to

                                        strike.

I am the MONSTER. I am the fright.

I am the haunted and the haunter
            the phantom lurking
behind a

mask

the ghost that can't be

busted

the monster that can't be

mashed.

The blood s u c k i n g vampire lusting to drain
                                        out
                                        your
                                        life
the soul that becomes a werewolf
      when the moon is full and bright.

I make the thriller.

  I am Friday the 13th.

I design the ghoulish grueling games
to play with your mind.

Seven days I give you
before your life is out of   time.

  I am the witch that cackles

cursing all your dreams

  I am your own precisely personal
Michael Myers on *Halloween.*

I know every scare
every trick, every treat

to send your mind spiraling
     down
       into
        triggering
         nightmares
         of
          deceit.

And though you try to run
though you try to hide

I am the IT, lurking in the gutters
waiting for you to pass by.

Journal Prompts

How much of your ancestors' trauma lives inside of you?

_____

_____

_____

_____

_____

_____

_____

_____

_____

_____

_____

_____

How has your mind been conditioned by others?

_____

_____

_____

_____

_____

_____

_____

_____

_____

_____

_____

_____

Phasing Freely

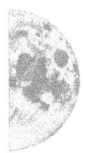

First Quarter

I am loved
a treasured
tended heart
protected by
parental life
doused in
bundled armor
cloaked
cherished
nurtured to
grow
ripen
progress.

Give me my flowers while I'm still here.

Marietta Woodson, my great-grandmother, radiated a captivating spirit, leaving behind a legacy of unique sayings and insights. Her wisdom is woven throughout this book and lives on in my heart. Her quotes will be distinguished by the distinctive font above.

Synthesis

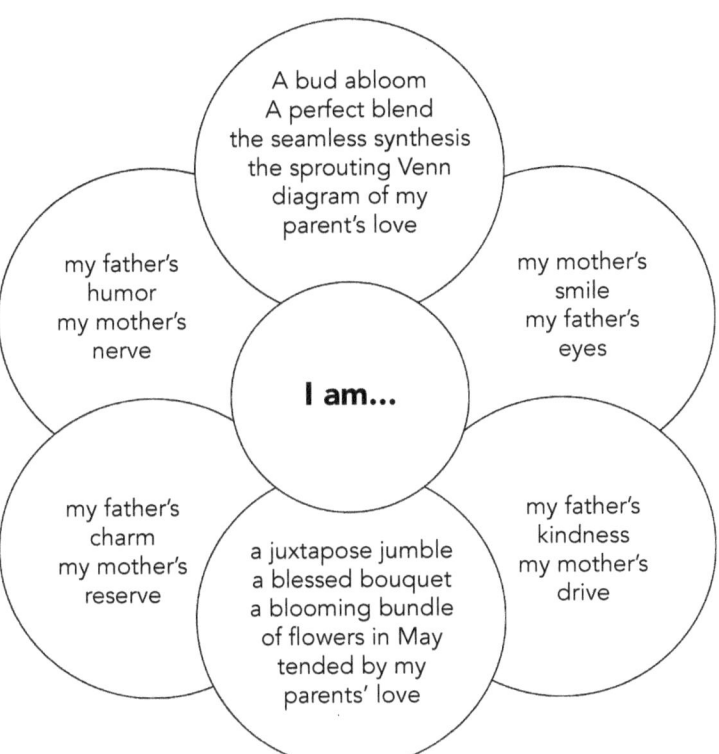

A bud abloom
A perfect blend
the seamless synthesis
the sprouting Venn
diagram of my
parent's love

my father's
humor
my mother's
nerve

my mother's
smile
my father's
eyes

I am...

my father's
charm
my mother's
reserve

a juxtapose jumble
a blessed bouquet
a blooming bundle
of flowers in May
tended by my
parents' love

my father's
kindness
my mother's
drive

Journal Prompts

Who do you need to give flowers to before they are gone?

_____
_____
_____
_____
_____
_____
_____
_____
_____
_____
_____
_____
_____
_____
_____
_____
_____
_____
_____
_____
_____
_____
_____
_____
_____
_____
_____
_____

Waxing Gibbous

I am consumed
a herded
black sheep
devoured by
alabaster life
shapeshifting
craving
belonging and
societal success
waiting to
shatter
explode
implode.

Swing

I used to swing

the entire recess
alone. I'd mount myself
on a rubber strap seat
grip the rustic, metal
chains connected to
aging, wooden frames
dangle my legs above
grizzled wood chips, and
push from my bony
undeveloped hips.

I used to swing

higher and higher, the
vast playground in my
sight. white classmates
scampered and scurried
gold hair matching the
yellow sun's light
white skin blushed
from running's might
just like the skin
I'd see on TV later
that night.

I used to swing

and watch the
jungle gym jamboree
as the popular girls
swooned over boys in glee
premature breasts bouncing
leg hair secretly sprouting.

boys would start chasing
girls would start bracing
screaming, beaming the
unnamed, instinctual
tension steaming.

I'd leave my swing

rush to the white
girl rescue and aid
kick, punch, pound the
air, a wild, miniature
Amazon saving white
damsels from their
white damsel despair.
the boys would scatter
the girls, flattered, would
smile and run away, but
no time to play with the
black girl today.

I'd return to my swing

and soar even higher
skinny legs propelling
Michigan winds swelling.
gripping the rustic, metal
chains, I'd push higher
until the wooden frame
screeched as I reached
the top of the peak

and then I'd release
suspend, soar, fly.
just for a moment
I was one with the
sky.

I used to land

on the ground
sink into the grizzled
wood chips, dirt
covered hands and
knees. no one there
to witness my power
just the hall monitor
stalking and watching
from her tilted tower.

I used to swing

the entire recess
alone. I'd mount myself
on a rubber strap seat
grip the rustic, metal
chains. the perfect
place for a black girl
surviving in white
terrain.

Tyler Lenn Bradley

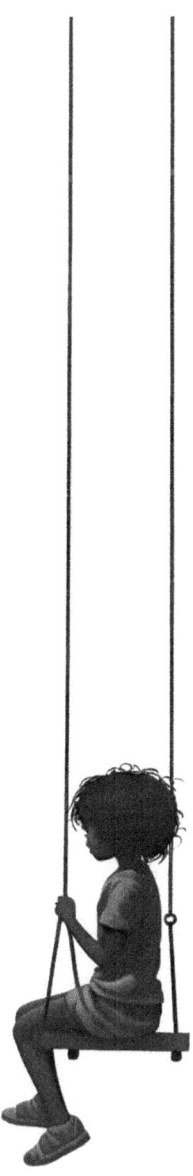

Consumed

white world white people white men white women white faces white eyes white beauty white thoughts white beliefs white opinions white ideas white dreams white nightmares **How much white do I need to wash out of my system in order to love myself?** white structures white companies white small businesses white corporations white schemes white lies white liberals white conservatives white elections white votes **How many white proclamations** white friends white teachers white colleagues white bosses white lovers white therapists white doctors white people on the street **do I need to evaporate from my mind so I can feel like I'm enough?** white media white television white movies white books white magazines white theater white musical theater white radio white news white stories **Like white out, this white world washes and wilts over my brown, black brilliance.** white drama white comedy white tragedy white commercials white marketing white spectacle white cartoons white animation white romcoms white savior narratives white documentaries white biographies white memoirs **Like white out, this white world has bleached my radiance** white mythology white fantasies white adventures white warrior white knight white superheroes white villains white rabbit **every inch of my hue** white fur white skin white hair white beard white bodies white style white clothes white lingerie **like thick glue it sits and sticks and spits on my existence, my mind, my being.** white robe white gown white wedding dresses white laundry white detergent white households **Like white out, this white world exists on every desk** white communities **every store** white neighborhood white house white ceilings white sidewalks white picket fences **every home** white granite countertops **every school** white playgrounds white colleges white universities white elite white poor white middle class **every book** white departments white faculties white academics white conferences white women seminars **everywhere, white is there** white summits white events white concerts white clubs **whether you can see it** white bars **feel it** white strippers **hear it** white strip clubs **smell it.** white sex **How many times have I nursed the white wolf in order to survive?** white sheep white dogs white cats white fox white bears white tigers great white sharks white waters white holy water white religion white church **How many times have I submerged myself in this white wilderness in order to thrive?** white santa clause white easter bunny white tooth fairy white father time white mother earth white gods white God white jesus white mary white moses white adam white eve white devil white demons white messiahs white prophets white saints white popes **How many tears have I concealed?** white leaders white experts white theories white hypotheses white mansplaining **Laughs I've faked?** white urban legends white conspiracy theories white magic **Words I've ignored to fit into this white mold,** white wizards white dragons **this white whimsical world, a wasteland for anyone who doesn't conform.** white dynasties white kings white queens white princesses white princes white kingdoms white castles white architecture **How much white wood have I gnawed, swallowed** white onions white bread white milk **drip by drip** white wine **drop by drop** white soda white rice white garlic **down my reluctant throat** white meat white fish white cheese **wanting to gag** white eggs **wanting to choke** white chocolate white donuts white cops **but knowing any sign of weakness will be my end?** white law white privilege white vacations white sand beaches white joy white guilt white tears white fears white love white porn white pride white washing **How do I wash white out in a white world?** white hip hop **How do I drown out the white noise?** white music white jazz white symphonies white rock and roll white alternative white country white soul white pop white celebrities white performers white actors white musicians white artists white dancers white athletes white models white geniuses white influencers white merchandise white video games white board games **Erase the white board?** white barbie dolls white baby dolls **How do I find myself in a world that wasn't made for me?** white toys white technology white phones white apps white websites white social media **How do I keep myself from being consumed?** white metaverse white NFTs white wealth white gold white limestone white pearls white diamonds white light white caskets white tombstones white clouds white heads in the clouds **How much white have *you* consumed?** white depression white oppression white pills white pains white pads white tampons white truths white history white philosophy white psychology white sociology white politics white politicians white presidents white mayors white governors white congressmen white economics white society white dominance white power white supremacy white nationalism white equality white lives matter white denial white flight white fragility white flags white colonialism white civilization white culture white customs white country white world...

Vital Deceit
Inspired by William Shakespeare, Romeo and Juliet

What's in a name? That which we call a rose
by any other name would smell as sweet?

What's in a name? My mom named me Tyler
so I would be hired, quite the deceit.

What's in a name? When you think of Tyler
what comes to your mind? What images creep?

What's in a name? When you think of Tyler
I bet your image is not my physique.

What's in a name? You see a well-dressed blond
white man, steady job with "normal, right" speech.

What's in a name? If my name was "Blacker"
would my resume be noticed or weak?

What's in a name? That which we call a Black
by a "Black" name would not seem quite as sweet?

What's in a name? That which we call a Black
by a "Black" name would not be seen as chic?

What's in a name? That which we call a Black
by a "Black" name would only be critiqued?

What's in a name? Everything. In this land
where Blacks fight to survive with silent shrieks.

What's in a name? My mom named me Tyler
a Black mother's plan, a vital deceit.

Conform

I used to write
with curly letters.
I used to flip my "r"
and role my "l."

I used to have swirls
curls all over the page
the joy it brought me.

But then, one day
my teacher told me
to STOP.
It would be too hard
for others to read.
It was too different.

Maybe that's the day
when I learned
to stop
being myself.

White Figures

Back to the Future your way into a time machine, turn the dial ever so slightly to the year 2015, and set the location to approximately 3:00 PM CST at one of the largest dance festivals in the US of A: a place where your worth is measured by the length of your split, the point of your toe, and the depth of your plié.

I, a non-technical, but passionate dancer had neither a split, pointed toe, or plié – but I had guts. Zoom in and you'll see me standing on stage in front of a full auditorium performing my first ever spoken word piece, titled, *Uncomfortable* and, boy, was I uncomfortable. Nervous, sweaty but determined, I performed a speech about social justice in a room with white walls, white floors, and a whole lot of white people. BUT my words were met with a standing ovation from everyone EXCEPT for two. Yes, two older white figures in the front row caught my eye. They did not stand or applaud with the rest. Instead, they sat arms crossed in what looked like a mix of disbelief, disdain, and disgust.

If you look closely at my eyes, you'll see my spirit slowly shatter.

NOW

Rick and Morty your way back into the time machine turn the dial 5 years prior to the year 2009, set the location to my high school at approximately 4:00PM EST and you'll find me sitting on the bathroom floor alone, fetal position, tears welling, punching myself in the gut, while rocking side to side after a tall, stretchy white figure told me that I wasn't good enough to join the sports team she systematically cut all the black girls from.

If you look closely at my eyes, you'll see my spirit slowly shatter.

NOW

Hot Tub Time Machine your way back into the time machine, turn the dial 8 years in the past to 1999, set the location to my elementary school at approximately 11:00AM EST, and you'll find a younger, braided hair version of myself eagerly volunteer to read a storybook out loud in my all-white, 2nd grade class. Watch as I excitedly waltz up to the front of the classroom and begin reading in delight even though I stutter and stammer over words with "s" and "t". Turn your head ever so slightly and you'll see a round, white teacher figure pounce over to me in disdain, rip the book from my hands in front of the entire class, send me back to sit on the floor and choose a white girl to read in my place.

If you look closely at my eyes, you'll see my spirit slowly shatter.

NOW, time to go WAY back!

Twilight Zone you're way back into the time machine, turn to the dial to I'm guessing around the year 1931, set the location to Tensas Parish, Louisiana, and let's just say 2:00PM CST and you'll find my great grandparents living and working on THEIR, yes, I said THEIR farm (they were the first black family to own their own farm in Tensas Parish).

Zoom in close and you'll see a white figure on their property trying to harass their children - my great aunts. But turn your head slightly to the right and you'll see my great grandfather, stand up to the white figure exclaiming "Get off my property!" Seconds later you'll see the white figure scamper, scatter, and run off like a deer in hunting season.

If you look closely at my great grandfather's eyes, you'll see that his spirit could not be shattered.

NOW for your last trip!

Manifest your way into the time machine, turn the dial approximately 90 years in the future, set the location to my apartment at approximately 11:00AM PST. You'll find me in a 3-piece suite on a work Zoom call -- the youngest, the darkest, and best dressed in the Zoom room. Listen closely and you'll hear the oldest, whitest, seniorest, and worst dressed white figure in the room laugh and talk over me as I try to explain how their idea may be offensive and quite possibly racist. Now inch a little closer and you'll see me, sweaty but steady, channel my great grandfather's spirit and stand up for what I know is right in a room full of white.

It took me a while to get there but –

If you look closely at my eyes, you'll see my spirit slowly learn to soar.

Scene 3: A Negro Woman

Setting: A Dream – YOUNG WOMAN's dream. In this dream YOUNG WOMAN comes face to face with herself, her mind – her ANXIETY and AMBITION.

Pages of a play script fall at YOUNG WOMAN's feet. Flickering specks of light shift from the outer darkness to YOUNG WOMAN as she examines the white papers. And with each page of the script, she remembers a new piece of a memory. She recalls this memory:

YOUNG WOMAN:
I remember that I was a senior in undergrad — a theater student – and I desperately wanted to write and produce my very own show. I had been thinking about it for years.

AMBITION:
And…

TYLER:
And one day I pitched my idea to the director of the theater department. He seemed interested, but it was really hard to read him. I can see him now. He sat back in his chair with a semi-sincere smile on his face. A white man, balding down the middle, with a resting face that combined pride, anger, longing and passion. He'd been at this school for years. People admired him, feared him, worshiped him. And you could tell that he loved it all.

ANXIETY:
[As the white man]
"Well, if you do your own show, you can't be

in my mainstage show. And my play has a **strong black woman** role that I think you'll be great for."

YOUNG WOMAN:
I was in disbelief when he said that. I mean I had **never** been asked to be in a mainstage show before. It literally felt like after five years of hard work, I was finally being noticed.

ANXIETY:
[as YOUNG WOMAN]
"Thank you for the offer. I'll think about it."

AMBITION:
And then what?

YOUNG WOMAN:
I left his office and immediately ran to the library to find this play. With every step I imagined what this "strong black woman" character was like. What was her motivation? Her desires? Her needs? The idea of diving into a black woman's story was a dream come true.

AMBITION:
And what did I find?

YOUNG WOMAN:
A Streetcar Named Desire by Tennessee Williams. I'd heard of it before but had never read it. In the Cast List I saw the names: "Blanche, Stella, Stanley, Harold, a Young Collector, A Prostitute, Steve, Pablo, A Doctor...and a Negro Woman."

ANXIETY:
[as YOUNG WOMAN]
"A Negro Woman? That can't be it."

AMBITION:
And?

ANXIETY:
And I began to think:
a negro woman
a token
that's all I was to him
that's all he could see.
Maybe that's all I could ever be?
"A" negro woman
Not even **"the."**

AMBITION:
I thought about school
and all those things my classmates said:
You're pretty for a black girl.
Can I touch your hair?
Why do you talk like that?
You don't act black
you act white.
Why are you angry, so uptight?
Are you an Oreo?
Since you're black
do you pee white?
Does your skin disappear at night?

ANXIETY:
I held that damn play in my hands
tears blocked my sight
so, I couldn't read the black ink
all I could see was pages full of white
just like my life
full of white:

White pages
White people

White textbooks
White dreams
White history
White movies

all while being
torn at the seams.

AMBITION:
And then…

ANXIETY:
I remembered
when I was a kid
and I realized one day
that my dad's eyes were turning blue
his pigmentation was wearing away.

And how happy I was to see
that someday that could be me
someday I could be beautiful too
like the prettiest girl in school
like my Barbies,
like the princesses I see on TV
so young and already longing to be
the opposite of who I was
the opposite of me.

YOUNG WOMAN:
A negro woman
that's who **he** wanted me to be.

ANXIETY:
And then…

AMBITION:
I held that **damn** play in my hands

and I made a pledge
that I wouldn't be his negro woman.
I would not be his muse
his token
his "check the box"
his rhythm and blues.

Instead, I would work hard.
I'd work so hard, I'd be the best.
I'd work so hard, I'd be better than the rest.

YOUNG WOMAN:

And that's what I did,
I worked hard and I produced **my show**
and it was good.
So good that people said it was better than his.

But it came with a price.
It came with late nights
no time for friends
no time to pause
no time to rest
no end.
Just keep going and going
hiding the tears
and, most of all
ignoring the **fear.**

AMBITION & ANXIETY:
What fear?

YOUNG WOMAN:
That **it** wouldn't be enough.

AMBITION & ANXIETY:
What wouldn't be enough?

YOUNG WOMAN:
That I wasn't enough.

*On the last "enough" YOUNG WOMAN's mind spirals,
spins and clashes as memories, emotions, and dreams
swirl like a vicious windstorm with no end in sight.*

YOUNG WOMAN:	*ANXIETY & AMBITION* *A continuous whisper that* *gradually gets louder.*
What's going on?	AMBITION: It won't be enough
Why is everything spinning?	ANXIETY: I'm not enough
I can't see anything…	AMBITION: It won't be enough
I can't think straight…	ANXIETY: I'm not enough
Answer me!	AMBITION: It won't be enough
Please make it stop.	ANXIETY: I'm not enough

YOUNG WOMAN:
Make it STOP!

*On the word "STOP" everything instantaneously
comes to a pause as YOUNG WOMAN's mind settles.*

YOUNG WOMAN:
What was that? What's going on? I want to leave!

AMBITION & ANXIETY:
You can't leave.

YOUNG WOMAN:
What do you mean, this is my dream…

AMBITION & ANXIETY:
(Interrupting) You can't escape your mind.

*Lights out. A keyboard appears in the distance.
Another memory. Another dream.*

One day a voice said
when asking about my dreams:
You'll get your doctorate degree

How do you know? I said.
You just will, the voice replied.

And without knowing why
I felt I had to agree.

Just another day where
unconsciously
my voice left me.

Expectations

To Do.

Long List
Short List
Lost List
Found List
Almost done list
Daily List
Weekday List
Weekend List
Long-term List
Short term List
Wish List
Dream List
SMART Goal List
Travel List
Check List
DIY List
Lists about Lists
Strength List
Weakness List
Appointment List
Work List
10-Min Task List
Inventory List
Password List
Packing List
Chore List
Fun List
Friends List
Family List
Call List
Love List
Gratitude List
Self-care List
Recipe List
Ingredient List

Wine List
Cleaning List
Laundry List
Homework List
Procrastination List
Due Date List
Honors List
Dean's List
President's List
Good List
Naughty List
Bucket List
Phone List
Best-of List
Watch List
Favorites List
Saved List
Reading List
Playlists
AFI 100 Greatest
Movies of
All-time List
Oscar Winner List
Billboard
Hot 100 List
BuzzFeed's List
Of 17 Viral Videos
Forbes 30
Before 30 List
Trending List
Follower List
List on a phone
List on a computer
List on paper
List in a journal
List on an app
List on random
scraps of paper

Lists hidden in the
underwear drawer
So many Lists
So much to do
So much to prove
But I can't seem to
Move...

Caged

Perhaps we confuse fear
with frustration. Perhaps
the dread and pounding
of our heart is not fear
but our inner child
begging to be released
from its confined cage.
A cage made from
expectations
pressures
and
shame.

In a small café in Rome, there is a woman...

she is beautiful, exquisite
a portrait come alive
a fair beauty, an archetype
of what I long to be.
she sips and sips
a latte with her dark
mysterious lover, staring
deep into his eyes. no
rush, no force
no lies.
and as she sips
my mind begins to
                              drift
                            and drift
                             and imagine
                              their lusting love.
                             threaded wool
                              falls off her body
                               drips down her alabaster skin.
                                his hands caress a hidden crevice
                                passion is the air, and no one
                                would dare end it.
                                     my drift
                                  suddenly shifts
                                  and shifts
                                and I picture
                              my lover back home
                            not dark or mysterious
                            but lovely in his way
                          but that lovely was not for
                        me. a love with no ecstasy
                    back at home where they always
rush
                                    and rush
                    no time to stop, to stare.

back at home where people
live lies and are forced to hide
their never-ending reliable cries.
I ceased my drift.
she still sips
and sips
and all I want
is to escape
my life and
live in her
lustful
drift.

Question 2

Q: What do these tears say?

A:

drop 1 – *I'm tired.*

drop 2 – *I'm trying.*

drop 3 – *I'm scared.*

drop 4 – *Please see me.*

drop 5 – *Please hear me.*

drop 6 – *Please help.*

drop 7 – *Pain helps.*

drop 8 - *A knife helps.*

TRIGGER TALES

ONCE UPON A TIME in a faraway land, there lived an enchanted trigger. It was a respected trigger, an accomplished, acclaimed, awarded trigger. The kind of trigger that others put on pedestals, the kind of trigger that others flocked to, revered, and believed in.

ONCE UPON A TIME in a faraway land, I sought after this trigger, desired to impress this trigger, learn from this trigger, be esteemed like this trigger. So, I watched how this trigger entranced and charmed all it deemed worthy and cursed anyone it deemed unworthy. I watched how this trigger proficiently and gracefully triggered tears, trauma, and trepidation day after day, hour after hour. I watched this trigger get away with triggering, how it's prestige and connections to other triggers were more important than it's triggering antics, more important than the tears it triggered.

ONCE UPON A TIME in a faraway land, I was the target of this trigger. I was its new prey. And with every triggering tactic in its might, this trigger triggered every trigger in my triggering body without control, consciousness, or consent.

ONCE UPON A TIME in a faraway land, I let this trigger invade my mind, gave this trigger power, let this trigger in, and my depression began to spin.

ONCE UPON A TIME in a faraway land, I almost gave my voice away, let this trigger lock me in its dungeon for its triggering play. But just before my story came to a tragic end, I woke myself with self-love's kiss and saddled my steady steed, slayed this trigger in its den and finally I was freed. And though it may have taken some time, and I let this trigger in, the moral of this story is…

I didn't let this trigger win.
And I lived mentally healthy ever after.

It's a funny thing living in a dark cloud.
Everyone expects you to see the sun because they do
but they don't have your eyes.

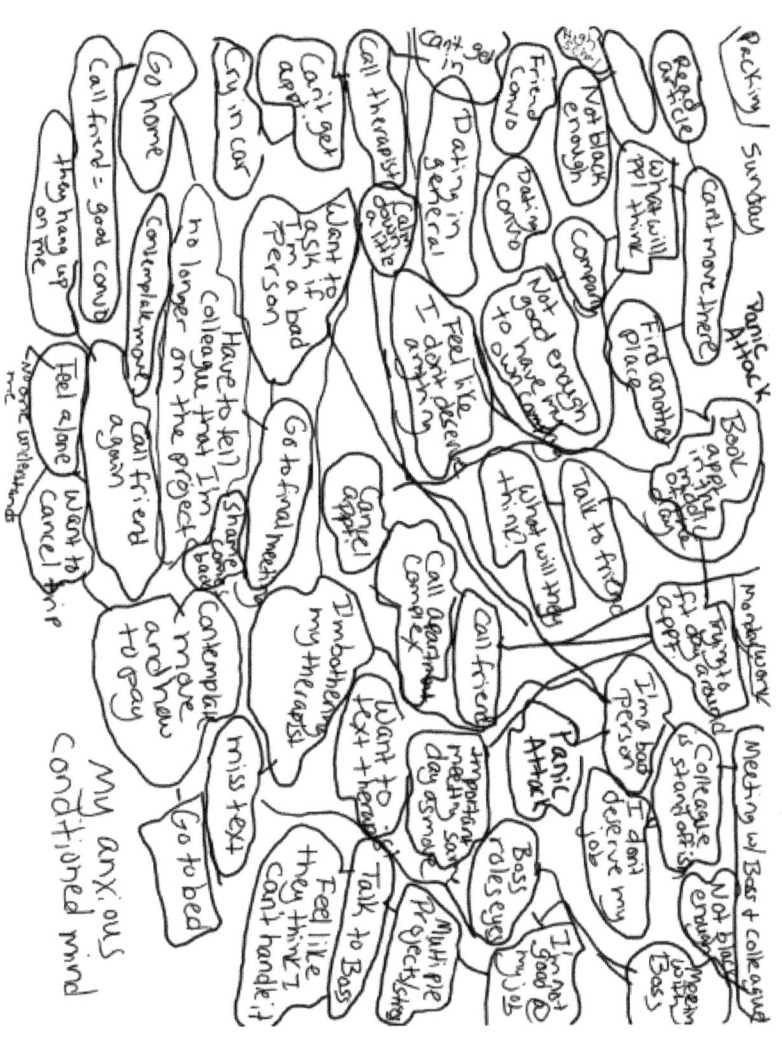

Journal Prompts

What expectations are clouding your truth?

_____

_____

_____

_____

_____

_____

_____

_____

_____

_____

_____

_____

_____

_____

What do your tears say?

_____

_____

_____

_____

_____

_____

_____

_____

_____

_____

_____

_____

_____

_____

Full Moon

I am exposed
a bare
naked
severed soul
a vacant life
isolated
unconscious
captive to my
howling mind
desperate to
let go
escape
fly.

Luminous Truth

On Wednesday, December 11, 2019,
at approximately 7:00PM PT, I stood
on a bridge with the desire to end my
life. But before I took my final step,
the Full Moon tenderly whispered:

I know your secret

        your truth. Calm

your manipulated mind –

        it possesses you. Stop

            your steps.

        I know your secret.

        I know all secrets

            for it is the night

        when tears   shed.

        It is the night

          when

lonesome souls – seek me

        as a friend.

Breathe

I know your secret.

This is not you -

this is not your time

not your   end.

Pause.

Remove your eyes

from the
beckoning

siren   cement   river

beneath you

a captivating canal of

chaos

Release.

Let the pain breathe

let it exist

so it can   cease

Gaze.

Not

upon me
but upon   You.

Marvel.

Not

upon me
but upon   *You.*

Wonder.

Not

upon me
but upon

         You.

    Look

     closely.

     There is
     hope
        here
     within your
     hollowed
        heart.

   Rest.

     I know your secret –

   the splendor
     that lives within.

       This is not your

   end

but a chance

to illuminate

your

truth

a chance to

Begin

Again.

On Wednesday, December 11, 2019, at approximately 7:15 PM PT, I walked away from a bridge with the desire to heal my mind and change my life. The Full Moon would forever be my muse - a luminous beacon of hope and truth.

Even when broken
we
still silently shine.

Journal Prompts

How can you find your shine when you're not feeling whole?

_____
_____
_____
_____
_____
_____
_____
_____
_____
_____
_____
_____
_____
_____
_____
_____
_____
_____
_____
_____
_____
_____
_____
_____
_____
_____
_____
_____

Waning Gibbous

I am evolving
an atom
nomadic molecule
courageous cell
dissecting
shame's life
unraveling
buried agony
gradually
abloom to
shed
emerge
manifest.

A daughter like me

I don't want a daughter
like me
I don't want her to struggle
like me
cry like me
look in the mirror, and
want to die
like me.

I don't want her to have
long nights with a knife
aimed at her wrist
praying for God
to assist
in her demise
like me.

Panic attacks with tears
hitting herself through fears
like me
listening to people
and their vile lies
hate her dark skin
and wish for blue eyes
like me.

No, I don't want a daughter
like me.

But, I want a daughter
like me.
I want her to dream
like me
see magic
like me

see the beauty
that others don't see
like me
to sing randomly
so terribly
sometimes even
unbearably
like me.

To light the world
with her smile
to follow her heart
and explore
every mile
like me.

Yes, *I want a daughter*
like me.

My future daughter:
There's so much
for me to do
so much distant trauma
I must unscrew
unpack, break the seal
so you, my love, can feel
everything that I couldn't
so *you*
can be free
not like me.

My future daughter
who will you be?
Someday I'll see
but first
I've got to love
me.

The Alphabet:
of things you don't have to be ashamed of:

Antidepressants
Boundaries
Crying
Depression
Eating junk food
Family
Goals
Help (asking for it or giving it)
Illness – both mental & physical
Joy
Knowing your worth
Letting calls go to voicemail
Mistakes
Not being okay
Opinions
Panic attacks
Quitting a job
Religion
Sex & Sexuality
Therapy
Unshaven [insert body part(s) of choice]
Vulnerability
Weight
Xiting toxic situations
Yawns
Zzzz – sleep!

Notified Worth

Am I defined by the red dot that appears above my feed? / How many likes? / How many loves do I need to feel like I am enough? / Is my worth defined by the number of notifications I receive? / Is it defined by the emoji-stained comments from followers, some I've never seen / in real life? / Am I defined by the number of followers I possess? / How many simulated friends do I need to not feel alone? / To feel seen? / Am I addicted to the dopamine? / To the rush of virtual validation? / Do I need to be notified of my worth? / Constantly? / Consistently? / Do I need daily doses of red dots to inform me that I belong? / That I am someone that deserves to be heard? / Noticed? / Desired? / Am I the photos that I post on the screen? / The filter cropped pixels / perfectly placed for praise? / Or am I the soul behind the image? / The soul so desperately in need to be worthy / of likes / and loves / from myself?

Question 3

Q: What if?

A: What if for just one day
I pretended like I was enough.

Maybe the next day
I would forget
I was pretending
and just believe it.

pLastic

Inspired by the film, Mean Girls

If Obsessive Thinking was a human
she'd be a Mean Girl
she'd be a Bitch.

She'd be walking around looking like a designer deer
in headlights - short skirt, high heels, doppler radar
breasts.

Picture this: you're just chilling, trying to get shit
done, trying to be productive and then out of
nowhere, Obsessive Thinking starts saying some
dumb ass shit:

Asking you ignorant questions about Africa
Telling you about her ESPN breasts.

Then next thing you know, you get NOTHING DONE
because you're too busy trying to stop Obsessive
Thinking from making out with her cousin.

I'm telling you if Obsessive Thinking were human
she'd be a Mean Girl
she'd be a Bitch.

Now if Anxiety was a human
she'd be a Mean Girl
she'd be a Bitch.

She'd be walking around looking like a designer
Toaster Strudel fresh out of an easy bake oven- short
skirt, high heels, and BIG HAIR full of secrets.

Picture this: You start hanging out with Anxiety and
suddenly you spend hours, upon hours, worrying and
freaking out about anything and everything: Jason,
Taylor Rodell, hoop earrings, Candy Cane Grams,
Brutus stabbing Cesar!

You can't even sleep well because you start having
nightmares of little BIG HAIR gremlins repeating:

That is so...Fetch, Fetch, Fetch, Fetch, Fetch, Fetch, Fetch,
Fetch, Fetch, Fetch, Fetch, Fetch, Fetch, Fetch, Fetch, Fetch,
Fetch, Fetch, Fetch, Fetch, Fetch, Fetch, Fetch, Fetch, Fetch,
Fetch

and finally, you wake up screaming:

"YOU CAN'T SIT WITH US!"

Let's face it.
If Anxiety was human
she would be a Mean Girl
she'd be a Bitch.

Now, If Depression was a human
she'd be a Mean Girl.
she'd be a BITCH.

She'd be walking around looking like a designer
Playboy Bunny, short skirt, high heels, nose job, just
looking to eff up someone's day.

Picture this:
You wake up, get out of bed
put on your favorite skirt
feel decent about yourself
look in the mirror
and along comes Depression and she says:
That is the ugliest effing skirt I've ever seen.

And you're like "okay, that hurt." But you just ignore
it. You go on about your day.

And then later, you decide to do something good
for yourself, you decide to start saving some money,
maybe pay off some student loans.

Then Depression appears out of nowhere in her
brand-new silver convertible that her daddy bought
her and she says:

Get in loser, we're going shopping.

And the next thing you know you're at the mall with
Obsessive Thinking, Anxiety, and Depression buying
pink outfits for Wednesdays because apparently you
must wear pink on Wednesdays!

But you let that go too. You just ignore Depression.
Go on about your day.

And then one day something great happens. You meet Mr. TLC
Mr. Tender, Love, and Care
He's kind, he's fine, and he helps you unwind.

But just when you think it's all going to work out, just when something good comes into your life, Depression comes along, steals Mr. TLC, and dangles him in front of you like a piece of high-quality meat that you can't afford.

(And you know WHY you can't afford it? Because you're too busy shopping for pink outfits for Wednesdays!)

on Wednesdays
We wear pink

But anyway -

You just let Depression do it. You don't speak up for yourself. You don't address it.
AGAIN, you just ignore Depression!

And ultimately, the only way you can get rid of Depression is if she gets hit by a bus, but even then, you still go visit her in the hospital AND bring her flowers!

WHY?!||||

WHY DO WE HANG OUT WITH THESE GIRLS?

WHY DO WE TRY SO HARD TO FIT IN OR HAVE THEM IN OUR LIFE?!

AND I'M DEFINITELY GUILTY OF THIS.

I've worn my short, tight skirts, walking around all prim
and proper like I've got a sock shoved up my ass while
singing "Jingle Bell Rock" off key.
I'm guilty of synthetically shaping
myself in order to fit in
sitting at the "right" tables
talking to the "right" people
just so I can survive.

BUT YOU KNOW WHAT?

I'm tired of Obsessive Thinking, Anxiety, and Depression.
I'm tired of living a life of PLASTIC.
In fact, I'm going to break this plastic.
I'm going to break this plastic, prissy, Prima Dona,
princess, prom crown into pieces, throw it into the
judgmental jungle of insecure society and be my own
Spring Fling Queen.

I'm going back to my old friends, the true queens, the
greatest people you'll ever meet:

The emo edgy, Fearless
and the fabulous
too gay to function, Pride.

I'll give Pride his pink shirt back.
Get back with Mr. TLC.
Book us all trip to Africa.

And I'll have myself a great time.
Leave my shark tank mind behind
and just learn to float.

I may even join the Mathletes.
It's going to be so GROOL!

Because you know what?

Obsessing over something won't make it go away.
Feeding into Anxiety and worry won't solve problems.
And ignoring Depression won't make room for happiness.
All we can do in life is try to solve the problem in front of
us.

And if the problem is our mental health
we have to throw away the toxic plastic.
We have to move forward
with
PRIDE
FEARLESSNESS
TENDER
LOVE
AND
CARE
FOR OURSELVES

The limit does not exist when we decide to
put our self-love first.

Now, I know I've said A LOT, but there are three things I
want you to remember:

1) Be kind to yourself and put your mental health first.
2) Being friends with Mean Girls is unnecessary and
draining.
3) And there's a 30% chance that it's already raining.

Which wolf will you feed today?

The growling	The giving
gnarling	gracious
grotesque	gentle
wolf	wolf
the blood	the boldly
thisty ran-	thriving re-
sacking vicious	stfully vivacious
wolf	wolf
the wired	the winsome
manipulative	moon-howling
mind sipping	mind shielding
wolf?	wolf?

Choose Wisely.

To: My Former Doctors

Dear Ms. White Gaslighting, LMFT,

I placed my trust in you, assumed good intent, depended on your credentialed expertise, and with vulnerability confessed:

Sometimes I feel uncomfortable around men. I've been grabbed, catcalled, poked, and stroked. Without warning, without consent.

And, Ms. White Gaslighting, you leered at me and said:

Perhaps, my dear, it's all in your head.

And I believed you.

Dear Ms. White Ignorance, OB/GYN,

I placed my trust in you, assumed good intent, depended on your credentialed expertise, and with vulnerability confessed:

Sometimes I have pain during sex.

And, Ms. White Ignorance, you sneered at me and said:

Your pelvis is too small, too tight for sex, but that makes sense. Your ancestors were from Africa, and had long legs for running, so there's nothing that we can do.

And, my dear, Ms. White Ignorance – on that day

I almost believed you.

Dear Ms. White Fragility, LMFT,

I placed my trust in you, assumed good intent,
depended on your credentialed expertise, and with
vulnerability confessed:

Sometimes, I feel like you don't validate my experience as a black woman.

And, Ms. White Fragility, your delicate demeanor
disappeared and with fragile rage you said:

I can't believe you called me a racist.

But, my dear, Ms. White Fragility - that's not what I
said, but rather than listen and learn. You
hung up on me instead.

So, I never called you again.

Dear Mr. White Privilege, OD,

I placed my trust in you, assumed good intent, depended on your credentialed expertise for restored vision, but instead:

You slid your finger down my body, copped a feel, a caress – a quick stroke.

Ironic how a doctor of eyes found his finger between my vagina and thigh.

So, I reported you.

My Dear Former Doctors,

Please don't misinterpret my words. I've had great doctors too, but unfortunately, my dear "experts," none of them were you.

Can you see the pattern? Do you notice the design? A domino effect engraved into the injustice of our time.

It's taken me years to learn how to defend myself in a world not made for black and brown people like me.

But that might not matter to you. Your actions may stay the same.
But don't you worry your complacent minds.

I will be the change.

With good intent,
Tyler Lenn Bradley, BIPOC

Note:
LMFT: Licensed Marriage and Family Therapist
OB/GYN: Obstetrician and Gynecologist
OD: Optometrist

Pussy Peace

Teens

Pussy!
Pure! Pussy.
Pure. Perfect! Pussy.
Pure. Perfect. Protected! Pussy.
Pure. Perfect. Protected. Prohibited! Pussy.
Pure. Perfect. Protected. Prohibited. - horny! – Pussy.

20s

Pussy!
Petrified! Pussy.
Petrified. Panicked! Pussy.
Petrified. Panicked. Private! Pussy.
Petrified. Panicked. Private. Pusillanimous! Pussy
Petrified. Panicked. Private. Pusillanimous. – impaired! –
Pussy.

30s

Pussy!
Peaceful! Pussy.
Peaceful. Potent! Pussy.
Peaceful. Potent. Plump! Pussy.
Peaceful. Potent. Plump. Pouring! Pussy.
Peaceful. Potent. Plump. Pouring. – imperfectly perfect! –
Pussy.

40s

Looking forward to it.

Scene 4: I AM

Stage right: YOUNG WOMAN and VOICE sit in a small 1960s décor living room.

VOICE:
Do you ever want to get married?

YOUNG WOMAN:
Yes, most definitely!

VOICE:
Well, he's never going to marry you.

YOUNG WOMAN:
Why would you say that?

VOICE:
Because you already live with him. He's already had you.

YOUNG WOMAN silently ponders this statement in her mind:

I AM   not to be had.

I AM   to be earned.

> My pussy isn't the end.
> It's just the beginning
> and if you're lucky to enter
> you better keep on giving.

I AM

A   good life decision
         long term plan

down payment
on a beach house
right next to the sand.

A   Roth IRA
        401(k)

        diamond from Kay
        worth more each day
        like fine chardonnay.
AND   I hate to be cliché
BUT   I am like Beyoncé,
        even when I stumble
        my Sasha Fierce will slay.

LISTEN.

I AM   not to be had.

I AM   to be earned.

        My heart is a PhD.
        Better get your doctorate
        in how to cherish a
        celestial soul like me.

IN FACT

I AM

        your recommended
        daily dose of vitamin
        C
        D
        E
        fresh off a fruit tree

pollinated by a bee
fuzzy, flying, and free

AND   any man would
be lucky to get
down on one knee
for me.

YOU SEE -

I AM   NOT TO BE HAD.

I AM   TO BE EARNED.

My pussy isn't my worth
it's just the beginning
and if you want my exquisite mind

YOU   better keep on giving.

*VOICE waits for YOUNG WOMAN's response.
YOUNG WOMAN has no need to respond. She
knows her worth. Lights out.*

Twenty Words in the last

Twenty Minutes of my

Twenties.

My Twenties were: Turbulent. Tenacious.
Terrifying. Triumphant.
Tearful. Thundering.
Theatric. Tickling.
Tense. Tattered.
Teeming. Tender.
Thrilling. Timid.
Tiring. Textured.
Twinkly. Twisted
Tasty. Thriving.

And I'm Thankful.

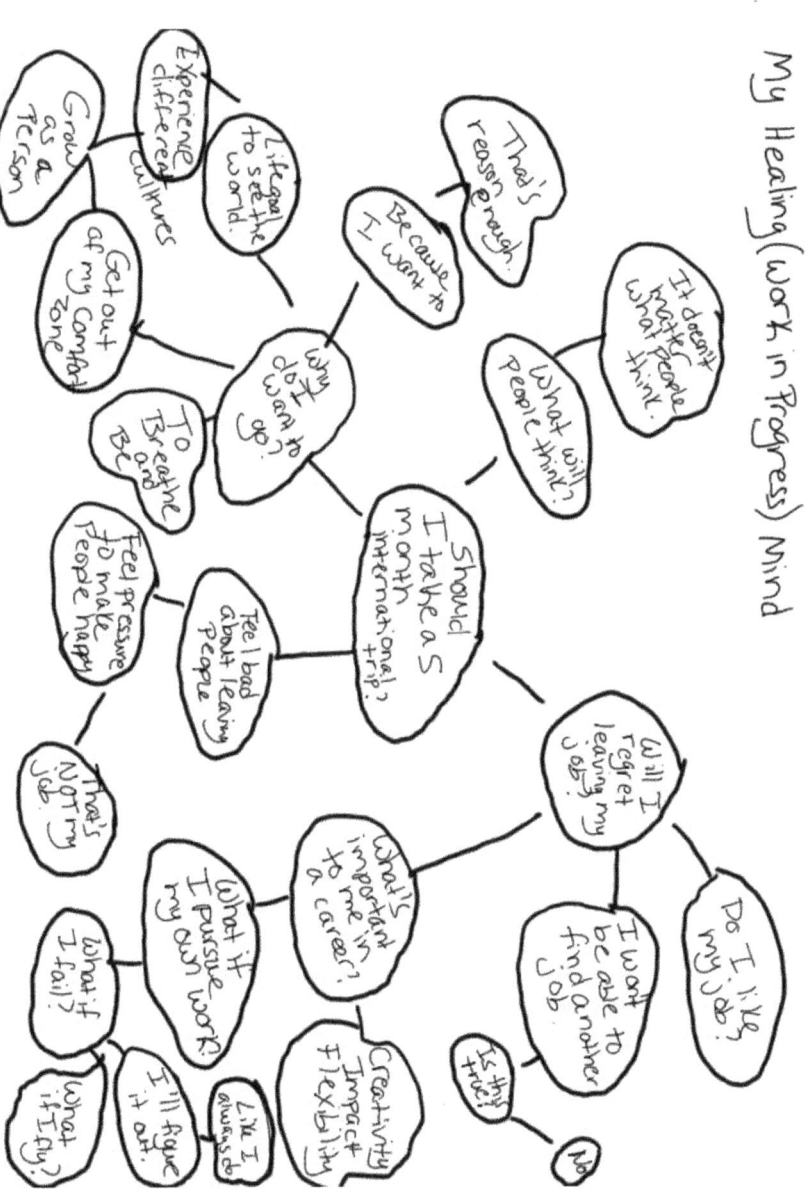

My Healing (Work in Progress) Mind

Journal Prompts

What if?

_____
_____
_____
_____
_____
_____
_____
_____
_____
_____
_____
_____
_____
_____

What wolves do you feed?

_____
_____
_____
_____
_____
_____
_____
_____
_____
_____
_____
_____
_____
_____

Last Quarter

I am beloved
a smitten
enchanted heart
captivated by
intimacy's life
smoldering
wildfire of
burning warmth
cherished
fiery to
dote
hold
embrace.

When asked to describe her late husband, my great grandmother simply replied:

He filled my little spot.

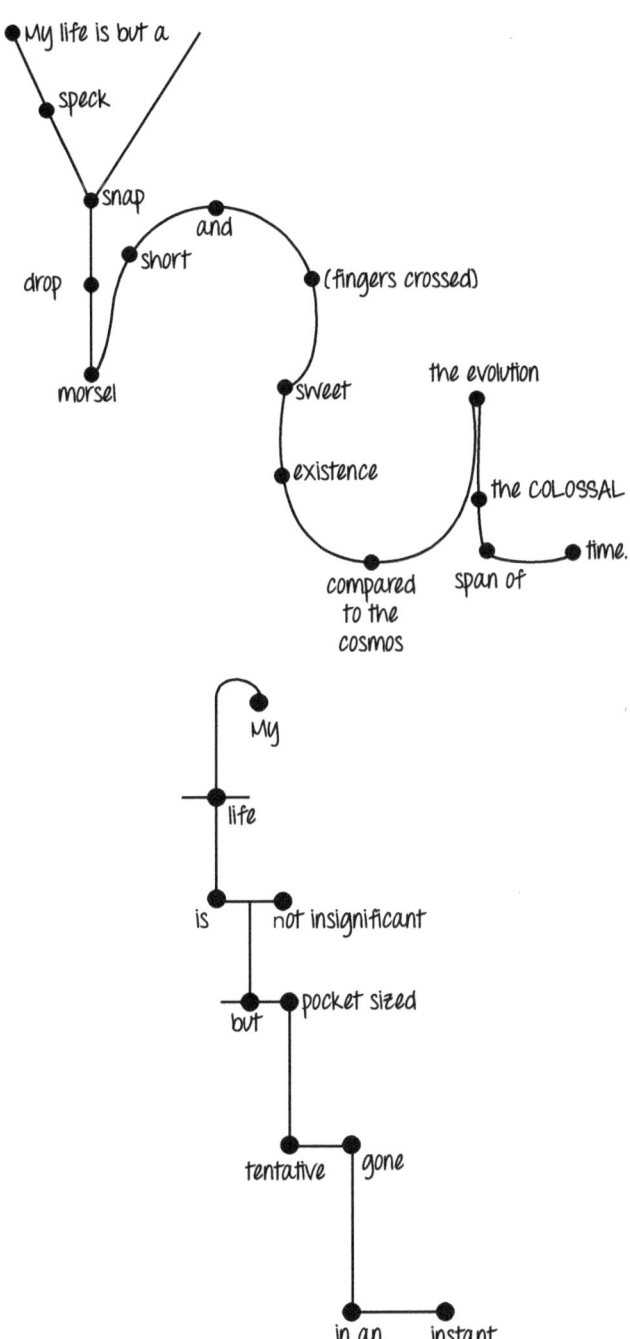

My life is but a
speck
snap
and
short
drop
(fingers crossed)
morsel
sweet
the evolution
existence
the COLOSSAL
compared
to the
cosmos
span of
time.

My
life
is   not insignificant
but   pocket sized
tentative gone
in an   instant.

Phasing Freely

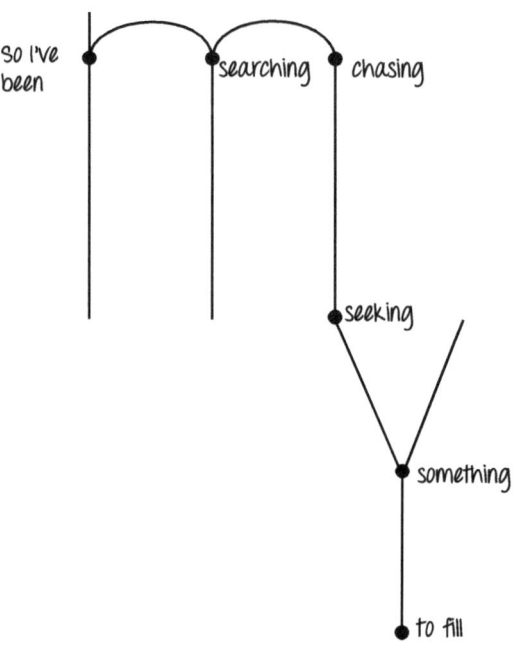

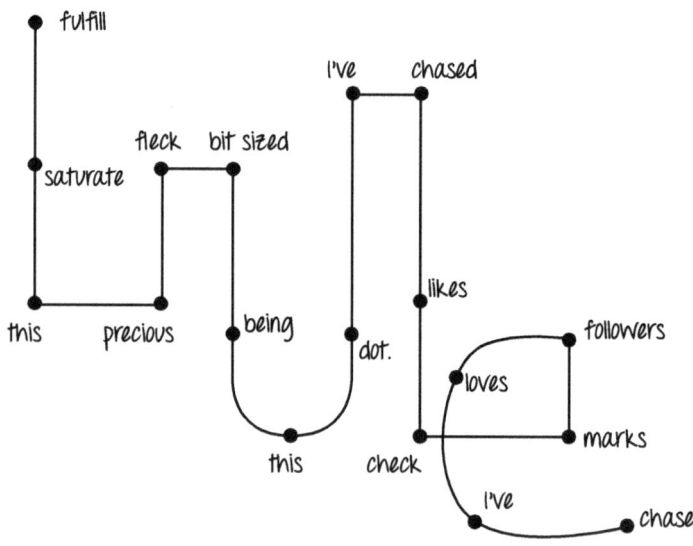

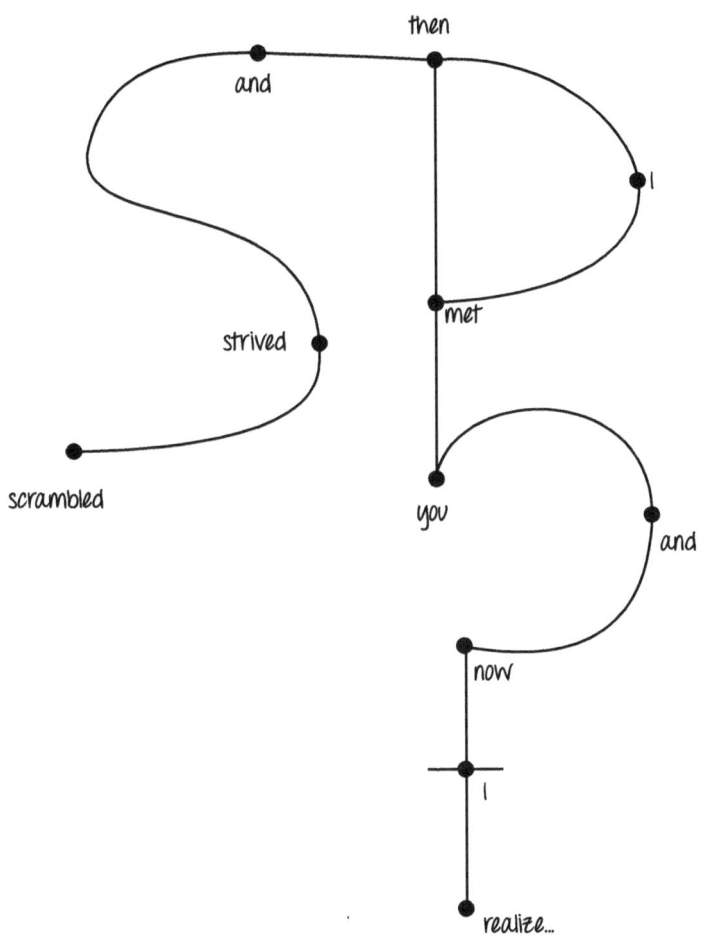

There is no amount of
accolades or success
that match the moments
when I lay on your chest
whispering sweet nothings
designing our own family crest
bold, black, and dazzling.
Together we will manifest
a life of exploration
a quest with finesse.

We lie entranced in sparks.
You kiss my head softly.
I trace your beauty marks
like a game of connect the dots.
I realize in that moment that
you, my love

you fill my little spot.

Journal Prompts

What or who fills your little spot?

_____

_____

_____

_____

_____

_____

_____

_____

_____

_____

_____

_____

_____

_____

_____

_____

_____

_____

_____

_____

_____

_____

_____

_____

_____

_____

_____

_____

_____

_____

_____

_____

_____

_____

Phasing Freely

Waning Crescent

I am defying
a timid yet
daring dove
braving
adventure's life
escaping
expectations
releasing routine
choosing to
let go
liberate
explore.

Promise to Myself

Dust, dirt, death - the inevitable
wooden box, six feet, a future I cannot
beat. But before my lights go out, before
the world seeps away, I promise to live by five
pillars from now until my last day:

I am only human.
I choose my own path.
I will be selective.
I will create radiance.
I am enough.

I am only human.

Breathe

Sometimes I forget to breathe.
So, caught up in the day-to-day
I forget to pause
to reflect
to look in the mirror
and marvel at my reflection
take pride in my direction
acknowledge all that I've done
and love myself
because I'm the only one.

But sometimes I forget to breathe.
I forget to connect.
So caught up in the pressures
that pile on my desk
I forget to look around and see
that the fate of the human race
depends on my actions.
It depends on me.
But sometimes I forget to breathe.

But beneath that shallow breath
is a mantra that I cannot forget:

Like a powerful wind swirling
through the dark of night
when I take flight
I bring magic to life
defeat villains
with the force of my light.

I am the architect of my life
the designer of my strife
and the writer of my dreams

And as hard as it seems
I will transform
break the norm.
I will ACT
and take the future by storm.

But sometimes I will forget to breathe
and that's okay
but I am only human
so I'll keep exhaling every day.

If I don't shit, I'll have to go to the hospital.

WOMEN SHIT

Yep, I shit
small round hard shits
long thick dick lookin' shits
hot & spicy shits
diarrhea shits.
Yep, I said diarrhea

and sometimes I'm
on my period
so I have bloody shits.

But guess what?
I'm still the shit!
I'm still glorious.
I'm still fine.
I'm still working hard
to get what's mine
all while taking
a shit
one *bloop*
at a time.

And if a man
has a problem
with that –
with a woman
that shits –

he can kiss my
natural black ass
that probably
just took a shit!

Yep, I'm a woman
AND
yep, I shit.

I choose my own path.

Ant Advice

While exploring a garden I saw…

an ant
 wandering
   through
     grass
       leaves
         soil
           earth
             as I do.

While toiling in a garden I noticed…

           so many
             paths
             twist
             turns
           decisions
         one   one
       corner a   corner of
        grassy   buzzing
       wetland   bees
     of small   pollinating
   crawling   floral
   life   life

but which one is right?
which path should I choose?

Pausing my toil in a garden I noticed…

                    the ant
                    was gone
                    decided to
                    move on

Phasing Freely

I ponder -
perhaps
the ant
is wiser?

For the ant does not toil or overthink.
The ant lives free and keeps moving in
sync with the earth.

While exploring a garden I understood...

paths are distinct
yet all full of life.

Any path will come
with both joy and strife

no right or wrong.
So, like an ant

just choose and
allow myself

to naturally
bloom

Different strokes for different folks.

Choices

There I was
lingering between
doubt and courage
tinkering between
stability and change
existing between
fear and faith.

But I decided not to choose.
Instead, I took both in my hands
and said, *let's go find adventure.*

I will be selective.

Selective Shopping

Don't go to the hardware store looking for bread.

Let me say it again:

Do Not go to the hardware store looking for bread.

At the hardware store you'll find practical and efficient *tools.* You'll find:

Power tools
Hand tools
Cleaning products
Paint
Utensils
Light bulbs
Duct tape

All sorts of tools to help you with your hands-on, pragmatic, DIY projects.

But you know what you won't find at a hardware store?

Bread.

BUT you *can* find bread at a bakery.

You can find all types of buttery, calming, scrumptious, compassionate, savory, empathetic, mouthwatering, soothing bread at the bakery!

I'm talking muffins, rolls, bagels, cakes, warm bread, cold bread, room temperature bread, flavored bread, bread with fruit, frosting, chocolate, vanilla, caramel…

(If you haven't noticed - I'm like Oprah in a Weight Watchers commercial, I LOVE BREAD!)

So, *believe me* when I say

You will NOT find bread at a hardware store.
I know.
I've looked.
In fact -
the last time I went to the hardware store looking for bread
I got duct tape thrown in my face
(it was quite the heartbreak).

Now, there are the occasional anomalies - there are the superstores:

the Walmarts
the Targets
the Ralphs or the Krogers
(depending on your zip code)
where you may be able to find BOTH – both tools
and bread –
and that's *wonderful*
BUT
most people are not superstores
most people can only either effectively give you
tools
or
bread.

Now there may be times when you might want a different perspective.
So, you intentionally go to the hardware store looking for bread.

Maybe you could find something close:
a candy bar at the check-out line
or gum out of a gumball machine?

But again, if you're looking for some good old,
home-cooked, fresh out the oven, compassionate
bread –

DON'T GO TO THE HARDWARE STORE!

Because let's face it – not everyone has the skillset to
give you what you need in the moment.

Some people are great at being compassionate, like
bread.
Others are great at giving practical advice, like tools.

Know who is who.
Know which is which.
Know what you need in the moment.
Be selective when shopping
and *protect* your heart.

*People will tell you what
you can or cannot do, but
the only one who decides
what you can do is
you.*

Gran Gran sits in the plaid upholstered chair
in the corner of a fancy New York hotel room.
Tomorrow morning is her son's funeral
but she has no memory of his death.

I sit on the edge of a firm hotel bed
dim yellow lights soften the room.
NBC news whispers in the background
hotel guests rattle the hallway.
It's just me and Gran Gran.
I like these moments.

Gran Gran asks me questions
the same old questions
in her same old way:
How old am I?
Do I have a boyfriend?
Where are we?
Why are we here?
I have to remind her
that her son is dead.

Gran Gran glances at the corner
of the firm hotel bed comforter.
The comforter isn't straight
she says.

I effortlessly rise and
glide my youthful body
toward the mangled sheets
but before I can reach
Gran Gran speaks:
I'll get it.

Are you sure?
I reply. But
she doesn't respond.

Instead, she slowly stands
from the plaid upholstered chair
her small, fragile body wobbles
her back hunches from years
of laughter and gumbo cooking.

Step by step
inch by inch
Gran Gran grabs and grips
ahold of furniture for support
a game of tedious teeter totter
until she reaches her destination.
And as she mends the mangled sheets
she speaks:

*People will tell you what
you can or cannot do, but
the only one who decides
what you can do is
you.*

Gran Gran makes her way back
to the plaid upholstered chair.
Where are we?
she asks.
I remind her.

It's been over 20 years.
Gran Gran is gone
but her simple act of
perseverance
her profound words
of resilience
will never leave me.

And one day
when I wobble

when I teeter
when I hunch
I will pass her voice
down to the next.

Wisdom.

I will create radiance.

The sun is shining on both sides of the house.

Atoms

Down to the atoms
past the years of
hate and lies

down to the atoms
past the divide
and the cries

down to the atoms
the cells
the DNA

we are all
just Human.

Maybe we'll
Remember…
Maybe…
Someday…

And it came to me
one moment:

I will forever
be learning
to love myself
more and more.

I will forever
be uncovering
discovering myself
more and more.

So, while on this journey
of finding true love inside
I will help others find
courage
to let self-love be their
guide

More and More.

I am enough.

Question 4

Q: Who am I when I'm not thinking something is wrong with me?

A:
I am of the divine
a wandering, celestial soul
the essence of freedom
co-creating with the universe.

I am a force
a velocity untouched
yet precisely balanced
in motion and ready to act.

I am an adventure
a courageous seeker
studious in the art of discovery
voyaging without fear.

I am of life
an entity of energy
generations of atoms
natures' natural dust.

Q: Who am I when I'm not thinking something is wrong with me?

A: I am just me
and that's enough
I am enough.

Ain't nothin' short about you, but your little toe.

My Self-Love Mantra

The warrior is me
the one that villains dread
the one called the dark knight

waiting
                        patiently

for the right moment to take

                                    flight.

I am the PROTECTOR. I make the light.

I am the defender and the damsel
            the sidekick veiled
behind a

mask

the captain that can be

trusted

the hero that can't be

smashed.

The web s l i n g i n g black widow fiercely in love
                                        with
                                        my
                                        precious
                                        life
the soul that becomes a Sailor Scout
when the moon is full and bright.

I make the magic

I am Wonder Woman.

I design the gallant, glorious gems
to infuse in my vision and mind.

Every day I avenge myself by
taking life one step at a   time.

               I am the sorcerer that soars

toward all my dreams.

I am my own precisely personal superhero on *Halloween.*

I *know* every spell
every trick, every treat

to send my mind spiraling
                down
                        into
                        affirming
                                self-compassion
                                        so, kind
                                        so, sweet.

And though fear is hard to outrun
though depression's reach is wide

I am the guardian of my galaxy
choosing to be brave and fly.

Journal Prompt

Who are you when you're not thinking something is
wrong with you?

_____
_____
_____
_____
_____
_____
_____
_____
_____
_____
_____
_____
_____

What are your life pillars?

_____
_____
_____
_____
_____
_____
_____
_____
_____
_____
_____
_____
_____
_____

New Moon

I am anew
a new breath
a new essence
a rare rebirth
reclaiming life
wandering eyes
selective
harmed
but armed
with self-love
waiting
to release
to become
to transform.

Be like the Moon

I've heard a great deal about the moon.

Small steps, giant leaps
blue moons without
a dream, while I sleep.

Mysterious dark craters
perhaps made of cheese
little green men
shadows to appease.

Monarchs, goddesses
wolves shaped like men
tales of death, lovers in flight
lust aroused by the moon's light.

Yes, I've heard a great deal about the moon.

Yet, no matter the story
the tall tale, the myth, the deceit
the moon remains constant
phases of ever-lasting beats.
Waning, waxing
no matter the riddle or rhyme
the moon is *itself*
now until the end of all time.

I've heard a great deal about myself.

Who I am, who I should be
what I can or cannot do
what I will or will not see.
Some voices are outsiders
others live inside of me.

Yes, I've heard a great deal about me.

But perhaps, if it try
I can be like the moon
and no matter the story
expectation, pressure, or lie
I can just be myself
phasing freely
now until the end of my time.

Dearest Human,

Thank you. Thank you so much for taking time to read my story, my layers, to peer into the window of my mind. I hope my journey helps you find radiance both in yourself and in others. I hope you transform into your own hero – the hero you truly deserve.

To close, I will leave you with one last quote from my great grandmother:

May you live as long as you want to, and may you want to, as long as you live.

Breathe & Be,
Tyler Lenn Bradley

P.S. You are enough.

Afterward

Luna, My Love
Lyrics
Written by: Tyler Lenn Bradley & Poet Hawkins

Intro
(Instrumental)

Verse
So many things are said about me.
Who I am, who I should be.
But dreams can't grow with weeds on the vine.
So, I make believe that the pain is fine.

Pre-Chorus
Weighted down
feeling low
but you fill the sky
like a marigold

Chorus
No matter the story
the riddle, or rhyme
your heart never changes
like people or time
the rise and the fall
the phase and the flow
but you light the night sky
and everyone knows

Tag 1
And I want to glow just like you
be free like you
Luna, my love.

Verse 2
So many tales are told about me.
Can I block the noise and just be me?
Fear comes knocking at my mind
but I've locked the door and I'll be fine.

Pre-Chorus
Weighted down
feeling low
but you fill the sky
like a marigold.

Chorus
No matter the story
the riddle, or rhyme
your heart never changes
like people or time
the rise and the fall
the phase and the flow
but you light the night sky
and everyone knows.

Bridge
Tear the darkness into pieces.
Let the tide take empty feelings.

Luna, my love.
Luna, my love.
Luna, my love.

Let your beauty be the lesson
help me rise above depression.

Luna, my love.
Luna, my love.
Luna, my love.

Chorus
No matter the story
the riddle, or rhyme
your heart never changes
like people or time
the rise and the fall
the phase and the flow
but you light the night sky
and everyone knows

Tag
And I want to glow just like you
be free like you
Luna, my love.

Tag 2
And I want to glow just like you
be brave like you
Luna, my love.

Acknowledgements

There are so many people to thank, so many who helped make this book possible and supported me through my writing process. A few are named below, but to everyone who I might have missed, please know that I am truly grateful.

Mom & Dad, thank you for your continued love and support.

My Family, thank you for your love.

Kevin, thank you for being my biggest fan.

Davina & Alegria Publishing, thank you for believing in my story.

Alex Petunia & karo ska, thank you for helping me find my voice.

My CLI Season 9 Cohort, thank you for your presence, we did it together.

Hiram Sims, thank you for creating a beautiful community.

The Community Literature Initiative Staff, thank you for making CLI possible.

The Los Angeles Poet Society, thank you for all your support.

Ann Marie Wells, thank you for your amazing editing skills.

Diane Castaneda, thank you for bringing my book to life.

Troy Mullin, thank you for helping create the book cover of my dreams.

Vivian Lee, thank you for designing my beautiful draft book cover.

My Therapist, thank you for helping me heal.

To ALL who read my book – Thank you for taking the time to read my story. I hope it helps you.

Author Bio

Tyler Lenn Bradley (she/her) is a dynamic poet, spoken word artist, and mental health advocate. Tyler strives to inspire others to thrive in the art of self-love and persevere towards their dreams with joy.

As a poet Tyler's work graces the pages of various national and international anthologies. In her debut poetry collection, 'Phasing Freely,' Tyler explores her personal mental health journey through the many phases of the moon. Inviting readers to excavate and examine the craters of their own lives through poetry, quotes, and journal prompts.

Tyler's poetry has a global footprint, having traveled, and performed throughout the United States, Italy, France, England, Ireland, Spain, and Australia. Her work transcends borders, touching hearts and inspiring minds wherever she goes.

For a look into Tyler's world of poetry, exploration, and continuous self-love journey, follow her on Instagram @TylerLennBradley. There, you'll encounter not just a poet, but a dream-chaser, who uses her art to encourage us all to love ourselves unconditionally.

Phasing Freely